Overcoming the Mountains

OZELL WILSON

Copyright © 2019 by Ozell Wilson
All rights reserved. No part of this book may be reproduced, scanned, or distributed in any printed or electronic form without permission.
First Edition: August 2019
Printed in the United States of America
ISBN: 1645504565
ISBN: 9781645504566

Table of Contents

Taking My First Steps 1
Conquering My Fears 4
Obstacles In My Way 25
Onward And Upward 29
About The Author 43

The characters in this story are real, but the names are made up to protect their privacy and identity. I would like to dedicate this book to my children and my very good friend Mary, who inspired me to continue on with my journey.

I'm opening this book with a prayer that for every woman that has an opportunity to read this book will not only be blessed, but encouraged in their walk through life. Whether you have given your life to God or not, I would pray that if you have not done so, after reading this book you will.

Sometimes we look for love and support through people and when we don't get it or that need is not fulfilled that void is empty. We long for love or some kind of recognition that someone cares, knowing that you are not invisible. Most of my life this is how I felt . . . invisible. I do not remember a lot of my younger years. I just knew I grew up with someone that my mother left me with. I didn't understand at that time . . . but now I know that the bible also states that all things work together for the good of those that love the Lord.

The scriptures go on to say God knew us before we were even born. So he had everything already under control. He knows everything you are going to go through.

And His word also tells us that he won't put no more on us than we can handle. When you are going through, it feels like you can't handle it, especially if you don't know the Lord. Sometimes even when we know him and have that relationship with the Lord; it still seems hard. And understand this; I learned years later as the Lord opened my eyes that it all comes together. I was not thinking about Psalms 23 or Psalms 91 at that time when I was going through.

God was with me every step of the way even when I didn't know it, and how do I know that? Because I am able to tell you today that you can make it through, God has your back if you can just trust Him, and he knows that way that you take. Trust him, have patience. This too shall pass, and you will come out of the situation with the victory. Let patience have its perfect work in you.

Taking My First Steps

After my mother had to give me up, there was emptiness within me that I didn't understand. At the age of three I was aware of the sadness in my life. Even though I did not know the Lord at that time of my life and believe that Psalms 23 was working mightily in my life. As time went on, not realizing the Lord is my shepherd, he was leading my life. And you can only look back to realize God's love was there all the time. Years went by, not knowing how I made it through, it sounded to me like a fairy tale, but now I know that dreams come true. Step by step, mountain by mountain Jesus led me through.

When I was 10 years old, I remember thinking in my mind what did I do to deserve being in this situation. I put up blockades, built up a lot of sadness and started searching for something. As time went on, I began to learn about Psalms 91 and that God had me hidden in His secret place, keeping me safe. You may be wondering how I could believe that God is keeping me safe when I my mother gave me up.

My biological mother had left me with these people. She was reallyyoung and going thru a lot of different problems.

She ended up meeting this couple whom she worked with at the time, so left me with them. Well, a little bit about where I was born.

I was born in Monroe, Louisiana. I was three years old when my biological mother took me to Illinois. In my earlier years, I don't remember much about my birth mother. The one thing I do remember is feeling sad. I guess you can say I started feeling unloved at an early age, not realizing that the enemy was filling my life with the spirit of rejection, loneliness, and insecurity, all of which is not healthy to grow into. I never stopped to think why my life seemed to be so sad or lonely.

But, I realized that it was the plan of the enemy for me to grow up insecure. Maybe not, because sometimes things happen so that God can be glorified. I do remember one thing that made me feel like someone cared.

My sister took me to a nightclub in Argo, Ill when I was five or six years old. I just remember someone paying attention to me. I had a God-Mother and a God-Father in Argo, Ill. They were really sweet to me. It seemed that most of my childhood wasn't very happy. But they brought some love for a short time just enough to want more.

I thank God for my birth mother loving me enough to leave me with someone, even if she could not have taken care of me herself. My life could have been a lot better; then again, it could have been a lot worse. Only God knows the path that we should take.

So the years passed and they weren't all bad. I remember one summer my stepmother and stepfather and I went to Louisiana. They were from there also. We went to visit her son and daughter-n-law. Her daughter-n-law mother had given her a live chicken. They tied the hands and feet together and gave it to me to hold. Now, remind you that I have never, ever seen a real live chicken up close, but they wanted me to hold it. So, you know I was scared, I sat back holding it as far away from me as I could. I remember my step mom telling me it wouldn't do anything to me. Of course, they thought it was cute. I was thinking what if this chicken poops on me?

Things were going good so far. So, as we were driving along, all of a sudden we hit a bump in the road, I was still holding the chicken. It started flapping its wings and in the front seat it went. They all had a good laugh from that. I didn't think it was so funny; I was shaking like a leaf.

We got the chicken home, and I watched my mother ring that chickens neck, the chicken flopped around for a while. I remember thinking to myself, "I was not going to eat any of that" (yeah right!).

I ate it, and that was some of the best chicken that I have ever had. I can't remember if we ate it the same day or the next day, but, boy that was some good chicken. A few years after the visit, my step mom's son Billy was killed. It was a very sad and strange time for me. Not understanding death, it seems even as a child I was very sensitive to sadness, pain, hurt. It has always affected me, no matter who it was. I never understood why I felt the way I did. But at the time I was young and did not know how to express my emotions. My mother who raised me was not the type of person who knew how to show love to one another. I needed real love and compassion.

After Billy passed away, she had a picture of him in his casket that she would keep out for everyone to see. I was afraid of it, well maybe not so much of being afraid. It was a scary feeling every time I looked at it. I really believe that started the beginning of fear in my life. I can remember many times as a child, my mom being at work, and I'd be home.

Conquering My Fears

Holding so much inside is so dangerous for us. When we are young and even when we get older, we take these things to heart and hide them in our hearts. Why can't we learn how to let go of the hurt? God started revealing different areas of my life to me. Each time we feel hurt or rejection all it does is add low self-esteem. Sometimes we wonder why can't I get free from this hurt, this pain, why can't I be happy and secure like other people, but God has given us all a measure of security in the form of faith. Hebrews 11:1 says, Now faith is the substance of things hoped for, the evidence of things not seen. Again, when you are young, how do you tap into that knowledge if you don't know about it?

To come out of being in bondage in your mind, we first have to take a leap of faith and trust God . . . that does not happen overnight. It took me years to understand this . . . and even now there are some areas in my life that God is still working on. I know by faith I will be made whole and happy. I have peace, and I am not nearly as afraid of things as I used to be.

In fact, know that God was teaching me day by day to take charge of these fears. I was not easy. The fear did not pop up overnight, and trust me it was not going away overnight.

I chose to step out and even now I am nervous. I will trust someone, however this time I know I will be more cautious and seek God for His wisdom and guidance.

Furthermore, there were some other areas in my life where fear showed up, when I started using drugs, alcohol, and men as a substitute to calm me from my fears. None of them really satisfied me. I was relying on my own way of handling the situation, operating in my own strength to conquer fear. When I began to read more in the Word of God about spiritual warfare (2 Cor. 10:5) on casting down imaginations and every high thing that exalts itself against the knowledge of God and bringing into captivity every thought to the obedience of Christ.

For God has not given us a Spirit of Fear, but of love, power, and a sound mind.

I started to think that my mind was playing tricks on me, because I couldn't understand why I was so afraid. All kinds of things just went thru my mind.

I had bad dreams of different things. I was really scared to stay alone, but I couldn't tell her that. As I grew older, the fear grew with me. I did not realize that it was just another way the enemy tried to set me up. I guess he figured that if he put enough fear in my heart that I would be no good for God. Because, the enemy knows better than we do, what God has in store for us? So, he tries to stop (hinder) that in any way that he can. As I got older we made more trips to Louisiana. I remember another time we went to visit, and this was long after my step mom's son had died. I was alone at her daughter-in-laws house. As I was sitting in the house already a little spooked, I couldn't figure out why.

At an early age, I could feel different types of emotions, not really knowing what they meant. I was sitting in the living room and I could see a presence of a shadow out of the corner of my eye, coming from the kitchen going thru to the bedroom. So, I ran outside, and the craziest thing happened. I found myself sitting on the side of the house, afraid to go back inside. There was a little hill there, and it had a lot of bricks on it. I took one of those bricks and hit myself in the head as hard as I could.

I know, sounds crazy right? But, I had no understanding of why I did it. I cried, and cried, and cried, I never told anyone about that to this day. Why? I don't really know. Probably because I thought they would not believe or I would be in trouble.

As the years went past, I never complained or talked about anything that went on inside of me. It just stayed there. At the time I really didn't know God, so I couldn't share my pain or hurt with him. But, as I think about it and think back, I realized that he knew me. How else could I have made it through all the fears I kept on the inside of me. God was with me, even when I didn't realize it.

I never remember having a birthday party, like most kids did. I don't even remember getting any presents on my birthday or if it was even being acknowledged, which was strange, but I had no recollection.

As the years went on, that was the most that I could remember when I was about 9 or 10 years old. We were living on the Westside of Chicago. William Penn is where I went to school. I remember it like it was yesterday. Going to this little restaurant where they had the best French fries I've ever had. They were the kind of fries that you get in a brown paper bag.

The bag would be so greasy that you would have to use two bags instead of one. After eating there a few times, there was this boy; I don't quite remember what his name was.

Everyday after school he would jump from behind cars, trees, bushes, anything, and scare the living daylights out of me. I was so afraid. It got so bad, that my mom and dad had to go up to the school and talk to the principal. I could see his face red all over, down to his neck.

He acted as if he was afraid also. After that incident I had to go and live with my sister for a little while. It was so weird that I don't remember going back to school. I remember when my nephew's went fishing all the time, and on a good day, now and again they would let me go with them. We used to catch a lot of crawfish, and we'd take them straight home and cook them. Those were some fun days. I remember seeing this really big turtle on the bank, as I got close to it, it didn't move. I thought it was maybe sick or something. I can't remember if we took it home or not.

As the days went on, this older guy that lived next door to my sister, he would always come over and sneak into my room. That's when he introduced me to different types of sex, not willingly.

I believe it happened several times, but even then I didn't say anything to anyone. After he got done, he would always give me a banana. I don't remember if my nephews knew or not, or if they put him up to it.

I just remember being afraid to tell anyone. I really didn't think anyone cared really, or even if they would believe me.

There were so many vague memories. Sometimes I felt like the different things that were happening to me, weren't really happening. It's kind of like I was looking in the mirror at someone else.

There were weird and crazy things that have happened to me as a child and growing up, things that I would never talk about out of fear as an older woman, it's embarrassing to talk about now. But to God be the Glory. I remember where we used to live, we had to go outside and pump water. We would usually try and do it before the darkness came.

We lived in a small town called Robbins; a suburb of Chicago, and there was a long dark alley from the pump to the house. There was this one night we waited until it got dark, and 'oh boy'! Why did we do that?

Through the years fear had already been a part of my life. So as we were coming from the pump, my nephew could see spirits, (at least that's what I was told). So, as we were walking down the dark alley, I was already spooked. So, my nephew who saw these spirits made a statement; he said "look at that man walking with his head in his hand?" Boy, what did he say that for? I dropped that pail I had and headed for the house as fast as I could. I was so terrified, I don't remember if we got in trouble that night for dropping that pail or not. All I know was I was scared.

That was a scary emotion and it stuck with me for a while. Where did all these different emotions go? I had no one to talk to or be honest with.

After so many years of keeping my emotions bottled up, if I did have someone to share them with, I wouldn't know how. I was unable to share my emotions with anyone. Growing up I really can't remember even having many friends. Some people would probably feel sorry for me. I felt like I was the black sheep of the family, so to speak. I believe that I was in the family. I just never felt part of the family. It's kind of like buying something for your house and just having it there, like a decoration, or its just part of the scenery.

As a child that is how I felt, like I was just there. I really never thought about it; I guess after a while I realized they were all the family I had, so I had to make the best of it. I never felt loved, not in the sense of feeling comfortable or really cared about.

I grew up with mixed feelings of what love was supposed to be. Its funny how we take things for granted and not understand a lot of reasons why we grow up the way we do. We tend to blame others. If God had not given me a new life and began teaching me what love is, I would probably be crazy or dead. Many people may be able to relate to these situations, or maybe not, but it's a fact.

Growing up as a child and not really knowing how to love or to be a part of a family, I find myself wondering what did I do wrong. I constantly ask myself, why did my mother leave me with these people? Every negative thought that the enemy threw my way, I thought it.

I didn't understand at the time. The enemy was having me think and feel so many unwanted emotions such as loneliness, resentment, and insecurity. That's the devil's job. He had a plan of destruction for my life, and I was on that road. But thanks be to God for Jesus.

As I got older, I longed to be loved and to feel loved, but in the process I just shut myself down. I wasn't a bad looking person at all. But some women use their pretty face and nice body to their advantage, but for me it was a disadvantage. I realize that now I was being taken advantage of.

It's funny how people stereotyped me, and how women used to see me and think that I was stuck up, or that I thought I was all of that, which was way beyond the truth. Truth be told, I never really stopped to see the true beauty within myself. I was so full of sadness, resentment, and loneliness, but no one saw any of that. When I came in contact with men, they just saw me as being easy, which is not how I wanted to be noticed.

When I started seventh grade, they use to have these little sock hops at school. I couldn't dance at all, but I always wanted to go like all the rest of the kids. My sister gave me permission to go there without my foster mother even knowing. My sister was my best friend, knowing that my mom would not let me go. I remember going to the school sock hop by myself. A few girls were there that I considered my friends; I could never remember their names.

I do remember having so much fun. A lot of guys were trying to talk to me, but I didn't know how to act at all. The attention I got from them made me feel something that I have never felt before, and it felt really good. After that night my mind was set on getting that attention, it's like I craved it.

I remember one time in Junior High, I had a fight with this girl, and I don't even know what I did to her. I don't remember what her name was, so I'll just call her Jan. She would always pick on me and say things to make me feel bad. Jan's parents would dress her really nice, and she was very popular. So, I wondered why would she pick on a nobody like me, I didn't have the nice clothes and shoes like she had, I wasn't popular. My mom bought me oxfords and I would get outside and put my tennis shoes on. I guess one day she made up her mind that she wanted to fight me. There was a girl that lived next door to me, her sisters were home, and they told me if I didn't fight Jan, she would continue to bother me. As frightened as I was of her, when it was all over, they were right. She never picked on me again. I was a quiet person and fighting really wasn't my thing. So, I was really glad that it was over.

As time went on and I got older, I started seeing guys that caught my eye. My mother was very strict on me, I could hardly do anything.

I remember her allowing me to go to this party. It started at 8 o'clock, and I had to be home by 10 o'clock. I told her it that the party was not over until midnight.

At the time I was about 15 or 16 years old. So, her come back was, if I was not home by 10, then I couldn't go. I went with this guy named Robert, he was nice to me and I thought he really liked me. Some of the guys that I met wanted to sneak around, but I wasn't always into that.

Robert came to my house and asked my mom if he could come see me, she allowed him to. It was just something about guys that wanted to do the right thing. I believe I was more into the ones that were already taken. They really didn't like me for me, as much as Robert did. We didn't see each other long.

The other guys were just into one thing and that one thing made me feel like I was loved. So, I really didn't care if they were being sneaky just to see me. I understood that it really wasn't me that they wanted, on the other hand; I didn't really care at the time. I was looking for something and really didn't realize how to go about getting the real love and affection that I so desperately desired. I was setting myself up to get hurt, time after time.

As I got older, I learned that if one person wasn't there when I wanted them, I'd get another one, that's how I dealt with rejection. I'd always tell myself that, "what one man won't do, another one will". I figured it was all a game, and there was no realness in it for me. That is how I wound up with all my kids. Today, I thank God for all of my children.

I started having babies. I had my first daughter in 1966. I had just turned 17 and was a sophomore in high school. When my mother found out I was pregnant, she put me out so I moved in with my niece. I had been messing around with this one guy named Jerry and for some reason we stopped seeing each other. Sometimes we want someone to blame, when the truth is, if you don't know what love is, you are just going through the motions. He was just like all the rest who had no meaning, so later I jumped right into the bed with another guy named Tom.

So, when I got pregnant, I thought it was this guy named Tom. For many years I believed the baby was Tom's, even though it really didn't matter. He didn't step up and do anything, but I guess Tom's mother knew all the time that that wasn't her granddaughter. She didn't just come out and say it or anything, but she didn't like the idea of me blaming her son as a father of my baby. She was a very beautiful baby with pretty grey eyes.

So, the years went on, and I stumbled upon this guy named Jerry, I was seeing him before I started seeing Tom. Jerry saw my daughter, by now she's a teenager. He told her that he was her father.

Oh boy . . . talking about feeling stupid, I didn't know what to say. As a teenager myself, jumping from relationship to relationship, I really didn't know. I was already pregnant when I stopped seeing Jerry.

Jerry and my daughter got along just fine. She got the opportunity to meet her grandmother and grandfather, so everything turned out good for her. After I had her, the babies kept coming.

When 1968 rolled around, I had another baby girl. Things had really gone haywire in my life. Everything was screwed up. So many things had happened at my niece's house where I eventually had to leave.

During the time I was carrying my first child, I had become acquainted with these girls that dressed really nice, they would go out and steal things.

At the time I was 16, and I had never stolen anything before in my life. So, we went into this store, and the other girls were sticking all kind of items and garments everywhere. It looked really easy, so with my gullible self; I figured I could grab some T-shirts and gowns for my baby. I walked around the store with my purse full of baby things looking for the other girls. They were nowhere in site.

Before I knew it, a man walks up from behind, taps me on my shoulders and tells me to follow him. All I could say was; "Oh My God!" I was so afraid and ashamed. They took me upstairs where they had already allowed the other girls to leave. My niece had to come and get me. The very first time I stole something I got caught. I went through a lot of trouble trying to do something because it looked easy and because someone else was doing it. That was the end of that. I never stole anything again.

Eventually I had to go to court, they were talking about taking my baby away from me after I have her, and putting her into foster care. My niece was nice enough to step up and say she will take my baby and be her guardian.

Ozell Wilson

My niece started getting public assistance for me and my daughter. I never complained because I was just grateful they didn't take my baby away from me. It was kind of rough there for me, I would hear people saying all kinds of crazy things about me for what ever reason. I cooked, I cleaned the house; I helped take care of her kids also. I did whatever I could to be accepted. After I had my baby, I wanted nothing more than to leave that house. I had taken all I could take. My way was being paid to live there.

I met another friend in Chicago Heights, Ill, where we use to go and hang out all the time. Chicago Heights is a small suburb right outside of Chicago. It was 1967, a huge snowstorm had hit. My friend and I had stayed in this apartment building. We went down the hall to these guys room, where they were drinking and getting high. At the time I didn't drink or smoke. So instead of getting up and leaving the room, I got up in the window, "how smart was I"? I didn't realize that all the smoke was going directly out the window. Eventually I got a contact from the smoke and started laughing out loud. I didn't realize I was high. Everyone started laughing at me also.

My friend and I ended up staying the night there. Soon, I started developing feelings for one of the guys named Jack. At the time Jack had two other women fighting over him, and both women had kids by him also. I realized that probably wouldn't work out for me.

I eventually wanted to go back and finish school, after I had my baby. I was only a sophomore when I got pregnant, and I dropped out. I really did want to return to school and finish, but it seemed to be a little harder than I imagined. I had to get up extra early and feed and dress my baby without any help from my niece. She wouldn't have gotten up and done it for me, so if I didn't get up and take care of the baby first, then I couldn't go to school.

I was late time after time, and after a while my teacher wouldn't excuse me anymore. There was not a lot of girls having babies and trying to go back to school. I was really upset with my niece that she would not help me out. She was getting assistance to take care of us, and she didn't want to go that extra mile to help me go back to school and try to make something of myself.

After a while I ended up leaving my nieces house, that's how I ended up at that apartment complex in the snowstorm. I moved in with a friend named Angel. Even still living with Angel, it didn't work out too long. More and more things happened at the house where we lived after the snowstorm. Now we both had to find somewhere else to live. Soon another woman came along she was kind of like a Godmother to me. She allowed me to live with her, her two daughters, and her son in a two bedroom apartment. The little boy had his own room, one girl had respiratory problems; she slept in a chair, and the other girl was usually gone. I slept on the couch.

In 1968, I had my second daughter. While living in that apartment, there wasn't enough room for me and my baby, so I couldn't keep her. She was a very beautiful little girl. Her father acted as if he didn't want anything to do with her, knowing if he did not want my baby I would just go off and be with someone else. I guess that was my way of needing to feel loved so nothing else really mattered. Eventually I got back together with him.

At this time both of my sisters wanted to take my baby girl with them which brought some confusion. I chose to leave my baby with one of my sisters, which was difficult. My other sister would always have something to say about what was going on with my baby. I was not sure if it was because she wanted the baby and wanted me to change my mind about where I left her, it was all a mess to me. My other sister always had a gift to see things before they happen. So she told me that God told her if they didn't stop fighting over my baby that he was going to take her. I didn't know what to do. I couldn't just get my baby because I didn't really have a place for myself to live. So I ended up telling my other sister that she could go and get my baby then.

The following morning before she could go and get the baby, I received a phone call telling me that I needed to get to the hospital because something was wrong with my baby. I got to the hospital as fast as I could, and when I got there my baby girl had died. After only 5 months of life, my sweet little precious baby had died that night from (SIDS) Sudden Infant Death Syndrome. My sister had gone in to get her up and dressed and she was not breathing. I was so hurt. I blamed myself and my sisters for a long time. I just about had a nervous break down. I didn't realize at the time, but God was with me even then.

We had a funeral for her, the father and his family was there. That was one of the hardest times in my life. I lost a part of me when she left. It took a while, but eventually I forgave myself. I know my God have also forgiven me. We have to forgive ourselves even when we have no control over the situation. It must have been meant for her to be in heaven with her Father. Whether or not I had my own place, and was able to take care of her, if it was God's will for her to be with him, eventually it was going to happen.

When we don't have Christ in our lives, the devil would just come in and put all kinds of negative thoughts into your head; but if you have a relationship with God, then you will know that every negative thought comes from Satan. I never really thought I needed to forgive myself after all these years, or maybe I did, and just didn't realize it. It's a good thing to know God, because it's never too late to repent and ask him for forgiveness. That is how we get free. If you repent and mean it, I guarantee, you will feel weights lifted off of you. I know I did. If you think you might be holding anything against anyone for any reason, it's never too late to ask for forgiveness.

After everything that's been going on, I ended up getting help from public assistance, they helped me get an apartment and a part-time job. I got into different trade schools, doing different things.

Things were finally starting to look up for me that was until I got pregnant again with my son. It seemed as if every time I looked at a man I got pregnant. Nevertheless he had another pregnant girlfriend. I didn't tell him that I was pregnant, the other girlfriend did. He ended up marrying her, but throughout my pregnancy we were still seeing each other.

After having my son, his father's sister and mother would keep him from day to day, accepting my baby as a part of their family. They bought him stuff all the time and never said anything bad to my son.

Kevin's (my son's father) sister and I became very close friends, as well as about five other girls that hung out together. We all started going out together, and every time Kevin's wife would see me out, she would always pick with me and try to start fights. I worked at a nightclub we used to go to a lot. I just got really tired of her picking with me. So, that night we started fighting, and I whooped her tail. She didn't bother me anymore. It was the second time in my life that I had to fight. Kevin would try and make me stay home, even though he was with his wife (how crazy was that)!

As time progressed, I started seeing this guy, which was actually the father of my daughter, the one that died. His name was Richard. Richard and I tried to work it out again. The year was 1971. Soon after we started seeing each other again, I became pregnant with another little boy.

He was a beautiful little boy, he had really long hair. Richard would always get mad at me for the simplest things, and every time he would get mad, he would disown my child. Richard's family knew of his son, but we didn't have that kind of relationship where I'd take my son over to see them. Richard's father was really nice, so he saw his grandfather a lot.

My little boy's hair grew longer and longer, so I decided to cut it off. Richard was highly upset with me; I guess I gave him another reason to disown his son. Richard had many other children, and baby mama drama, so my son and I just kind of stayed out of his way. Eventually, I got on birth control, started back working and took up another trade.

I learned how to type training in the Mayor's office. It was a nice day I decided to wear this really nice blouse to work. It was the kind of blouse that you didn't need a bra with. For some reason the women there didn't like me, I guess that put the icing on the cake wearing that blouse to work. The older women didn't like it, they turned their nose up at me; they snickered and whispered behind my back. I was the only black woman working there at the time. Eventually I was told to sit in the back of the office where I couldn't see anything. I was a very nice looking young lady in my early twenties, with a nice build. No matter what I did, those women tried to use any and everything against me.

Somehow they convinced the boss to come and tell me that I needed to go home and change my blouse. Even though he said he didn't see anything wrong with it, it's just that the other women didn't like it. I ended up leaving there. I had another job at a nightclub. I worked there for a while. Things were looking pretty good for me. I had a nice apartment, and my boys were doing extremely well. Then, one day out the blue, someone sent child welfare to my house saying I wasn't feeding or taking care of my boys. That was all a big misunderstanding.

My house was always clean, my boys were always clean. I've been around and seen what it's like for children to live in dirty and unpleasant houses, and I would never want that for my children. Anyone that knew me knew I took good care of my kids. I found out that another woman was jealous because her man was looking at me. So, when the people came to my house, I had all the linen off the beds. I had just returned home from washing. The clothes were folded and there was food in the refrigerator.

I inquired about where they had gotten their information, but of course they wouldn't tell me, even though I had already figured it out. To God be the glory they found out it was all just a lie. They closed the case immediately.

As I become older and older I realize people were trying to get me into trouble my whole life. Some of it I surrendered to, and other times I held my ground. Most of it was a jealousy thing. Jealousy is a dangerous spirit. God is good. My life was good. I'd go to work and return home to be with my boys.

I remember getting off work, and this man was following me. It was a warm summer night. I stopped to talk to one of my girlfriends, just to buy some time until that guy left. So, I continued my journey home, he continued to follow me, I guess he watched me the whole time. A lot of times I would walk home if I didn't have a ride. I had on this really nice and fitted hot pants ensemble.

As I started to walk up my back staircase, he came up from behind holding a gun. I was terrified; I didn't know what to do. He walked me back to his car holding the gun to my back, and warned me if I scream;

I would never see my kids again. I figured it must have been someone that knew me to know I had kids.

After a journey to his car, he raped me and took all the money I made in tips from work. I called the police and made a report, they never found the guy. I went to the hospital to get checked out. Now I blamed myself for what happened, due to the outfit I had worn. Trust me I never wore that outfit again, or anything that revealing anywhere.

For a long time as I walked down the street, I would always continue to watch behind me even during the day. Every man I saw resembled him. After what happened that day; my life was never the same. If I didn't have a ride to or from work at night, I just wouldn't work. I'm not sure how many people really realize how fear can fester into one's life, and spark all kinds of problems. It was not until I joined church during a deliverance service that I gave my life up to God and I was free from that bondage.

We can be afraid of all kinds of things and not understand why. I used to be afraid of being home alone, but after I started attending church services and when my kids started leaving home one by one, I did not know what I was going to do. I understood that there were spirits that I had to be delivered from. Every night the enemy would bring fear into me as I was praying. I felt something in my room. The Holy Spirit started pleading the blood of Jesus through my spirit. I found myself repeating it out loud. "The Blood of Jesus" "The Blood of Jesus"

As I sat up in my bed that night and proclaimed to the enemy that this is my house, and you have no right to be here. There was such a peace that came upon me. After that I looked forward to my house being peaceful and quiet. "Praise God another mountain that I have overcome."

I did not get deliverance from fear until I moved away from the state of Illinois. I realize as long as we do what the enemy wants us to do; being afraid was the farthest thing from our minds. As soon as I allowed God to turn my life around; everything came to the surface. The devil knows how to confuse us. Think about this – when we were not saved, we would walk the streets at night and never be afraid. But as soon as you get saved, you have to be in the house before it gets dark.

Life was getting better, my boys were getting bigger and we still had a nice place to live. I continued to work in bars, because I made really good money from tips. I hung out with another group of girls, consisting of partying at clubs every weekend. One night I ended up going out with this DJ that worked at the club we attended. They had a panamazing contest every Thursday. Panamazing is what they call karaoke today. My girls and I would all get together and hang out.

Our goal was to win, at least one of us. We would all decide what each one of us was going to do before we got there. As terrified as I was, I did what I had in mind to do, and I actually won a round of drinks. We drank all night, and we had a great time. I continued to see the DJ for a while, but it didn't last long. I had an eye for the owner's nephew. Eventually I was seeing them both. For some reason I could never stay with one man for too long. Again, I started seeing this other guy, he was a little younger that I was.

Still, in my early twenties, I didn't know what I was doing, still looking for love in all the wrong places. I knew eventually I would have to let him go. One weekend at the club, he was seen with another woman. I didn't get upset or anything I just kept dancing and having myself a good time. He had been drinking, and so was I.

But, for some reason he kept sliding to the front of the club where I was, trying to tell me who I can dance with and who I couldn't dance with. I didn't pay him any attention, I simply told him to go back to his girlfriend; "I'm done with you"!

He turned around and prepared himself to leave my presence. The next thing I knew; I saw strobe lights directly in my face. The DJ decided to play childish games with me, because I didn't show him any attention. What did he expect me to do?

I wasn't just going to sit there and allow him to prance around in my face with another girl. I told the girls that I was with, that if this man continues to bother me; I was going to do something to him, just to get him to leave me alone. Soon someone passed me a knife, I wasn't a violent person, and I just wanted him to leave me alone.

As he got ready to leave to the club, he walked past me and hit me in the head with a bag. I'm not sure what was in the bag; it couldn't have been much because it didn't hurt. I guess he wanted me too see him leave with this young girl.

By this time I was pissed, not because of him and the other girl, but because he just wouldn't leave me alone. I believe I pissed him off more by just ignoring him.

So, after that I jumped up and got behind him, tapped him on his shoulders; when he turned around I tried to stab him in his arm, instead it penetrated into his chest and punctured his lungs. I guess if he hadn't been drinking he may have died. I thank God he didn't. He didn't press charges against me, nor did his uncle, because his uncle had been watching him. The state of Illinois decided to pick up the charge, and I had to spend the weekend in the county jail. One of my aunt's came to see me while I was there, but it was nothing they could do for me. I cried like a baby.

I didn't know the Lord at that time, but he was right there with me. I came in contact with the judicial system a few years earlier when I got caught stealing.

Even though I only spent maybe an hour in the county at the time; this was something different, I had to spend the whole weekend incarcerated. I have never been in jail. The people there were nice to me; I even had a young lady there braid my hair. I later on heard through the grapevine that I was being set up; I guess they figured I'd be there for a while.

Monday morning came around and I went to court. The guy was there out of the hospital with his uncle, and he was doing just fine. All of the charges were dropped against me. I guess the officers filed the charges not realizing if the man would live or die. But, I just thank God he survived and didn't press charges. I don't know if I could live with the fact that he could have died.

After that the guy was afraid of me; for a while he didn't want to be in my presence. I wasn't the person he thought I was. I always found myself in the weirdest positions, only trying to protect myself. I wasn't a violent person, not at all.

Sometimes you get backed into a corner and it seems like the only way out is to fight, but that was not the right thing to do. Once again my God bought me through. I started dating older men. I enjoyed the fact that they would buy me things; like clothes, and shoes, and even just give me money so I wouldn't be broke. I felt I was doing awesome, but that didn't stop me from still seeing guys in my age group. The guys that were my age were my party friends.

Growing up in the early 70's and 80's; partying like we did, I was introduced to all kinds of drugs, pills, anything you can think of and I tried them all. I remember one night while partying I slipped up and tried LSD. It made me hallucinate, and that was from just half of the pill. I don't even remember who I got the pill from. I really can't remember half the things in my lifetime, or what happened, sometimes as I sit back and think most things comes to my remembrance.

When I think about it, the enemy has tried to take me out my entire life one way or the other. After I took that pill I just sat on the barstool for a long time so frightened to move. When I finally got the nerve to move, I ended up at home, how I got there; I have no idea! As I think back, and remember some of the people that I took LSD with; half of them lost their minds or their lives in the process.

I thank God because I know it wasn't me that was keeping me alive. Even though I didn't attend any church services at the time, I still prayed every day and night to God. As I got older, I wondered why my mom had to give me away. Of course, the enemy had me thinking it was my entire fault. It had me thinking I wasn't good enough, or I was a bad person, which bought me more spirits of resentment.

I prayed to God every night to allow me to see my biological mother, just to ask her what I had done and how come she didn't want me. I would ask God to show me who I was and where did I come from? There was such a void in my life, and I was just trying to fulfill it.

At this point and time I was living with one of my stepsisters. Most of them went to this Baptist church. Eventually I was lead to go with them, and I can admit it really felt good going to church. I ended up joining the choir, and had the chance to lead a song. The feeling I received was indescribable. Something happened while living with my stepsister, and I went back home with my mother.

My mother didn't allow me to go to church. I didn't realize that church is where I should've been all these years. I guess my mother felt since she didn't go to church, I wasn't allowed to.

A few years passed and I started dating another guy. It was never a love thing with him, just pretty much lusting to feel loved. I never knew what love was anyway. My family didn't show me much love; I knew in my heart that I was missing something, and I wasn't going to stop until I found it. I was constantly looking in all the wrong places. I used to feel like throughout all the men I've dated; somebody really cared; I like to think they did anyway. Thinking to myself, I'm not sure if I really cared.

The thing of it is this, having a hole in your heart and realizing that something is missing, but not knowing what it is, was hard to try and repair. I'm realizing that a person can't fix a problem if they don't know what's broken. Only God could fix it.

The birth control that I was taking was making me sick. I had to stop taking them. I was pregnant once again for the fourth time, with another little girl. And yes, of course he had another woman, and she was not very happy. As you can see, just about every guy I ever dated I ended up pregnant by had another girlfriend somewhere.

I guess you can say he was trying to be a father to my daughter. He bought a lot of clothes and things for my daughter; meanwhile his girlfriend was trying to figure out where I lived. That is what he had told me.

For a while I couldn't understand why she wanted to know where I lived. I realized it when I went to work one night and came home; my house had been broken into, all kinds of things were taken; even my baby clothes and things she had just gotten. My daughter's father bought all the things back that his girlfriend had stolen. She must have been upset that he and I were still seeing each other after I had my baby. I called the police and filed a report on her for breaking into my house and stealing my things.

We proceeded to court; she was making all kinds of loud outbursts at me, using foul language and everything. Now we were in the courtroom, and I really didn't want any drama with her, I just wanted her to leave me alone. I did blurt out that she was just jealous because I was pregnant by Ronald; my daughter's father and her boyfriend. That started a huge fight inside the courthouse.

We were both locked up for disorderly conduct. I had money at home, so I had a friend go to my house and get my money so I can bond out. The other woman didn't post bail until later on that evening. The year was 1976. I was in the process of getting another apartment.

During my boys summer break, my stepmother took them down south to Louisiana with her. I can't remember if she had moved back there or if she was just visiting. So when the other woman finally got out of jail, she came over to one of my friend's house because she knew I'd always be there. I guess being in jail didn't help her calm down at all, it made her more furious.

One night I decided to go to a motel with Ronald; I really didn't feel comfortable sleeping with guys at my friend's house. He didn't have a car at the time, so he use to drive his other girlfriends car. She must have spotted her car at the motel, how she found out what room we were in was still a mystery to me. When he realized it was her at the door, he whispered for me to take a cab home. Finally she got into the room, and she charged at me, we tossed and turned for a while with him in the middle. Ronald and I still continued to see each other.

After I had my baby girl, that women pranced around town making rumors that her boyfriend wasn't my daughter's father. This one older woman knew my daughter's grandmother before she passed away; she actually took up for me saying that my daughter looked exactly like her grandmother. Before the guy's girlfriend died she had the chance to visit with my daughter and really acknowledge that she was her boyfriends.

So when she passed away my daughter wanted to be there for her father. Even though things weren't that well between them, I allowed her to attend the service. I escorted her to the funeral, after that I believe her father had a little more respect for her. By this time I wasn't seeing him anymore.

The following year rolled and I met Jack; another man with drama; and more kids. And of course I had another little precious girl. I was trying to get my life back on track with working and everything.

Within the next three years I had two more kids, another girl, and another boy. By this time I was a little disgusted with myself. I loved my children dearly, but I was having them way too fast, and it was starting to bother me.

I came in contact with another guy named Rick. It was a little different with him; we had been seeing each other for a while. Rick eventually bought his son over to meet me; he was about 19 years old. Rick had been living with another woman, and decided to abort the relationship he had with her and wanted to move in with me. I had never had a man to live with me, so this was all new to me. He left my place in route to his house to get his things. I didn't know at the time that he was wanted by the police, being involved in lots of illegal things. The other woman called the police on him.

I guess she was mad that he was leaving her for me; he was caught and arrested, sentenced to life in prison.

I was pregnant again for the last time. My life was a big mess. My boys had gotten older; I guess they realized how old they were and one of them decided to rob a money truck with some other boys. I had too many kids now for the little apartment I was in, so eventually we had to move to a bigger spot. I had so much going on at one time; I just couldn't deal with another child. I decided I was going to give my baby up for an adoption.

I made a choice that I will regret for the rest of my life. I had been thrown fast balls, and curve balls my entire life, what was I to do? I had no one to help me through this, or to keep me from making decisions that I later regret. I made a lot of stupid decisions, but the decision I made to give my baby away was the worst.

It was really hard, early in my years I lost a child due to (SIDS) now I had to give one away. One of my sister's ended up taken her in, which was good because she stayed in the family. She's grown up to be a beautiful young lady with two little boys of her own. I tried to explain to her why I had to give her up and the situations I was faced with. I believe she understood, but not enough to continue to wonder why her, and not the rest.

It was just that she was the last one. I was just going through so much that I was afraid I couldn't even take good care of another little baby. I had to do what was best for them.

I can truly say I understood how she felt, because I dealt with the same thing, my biological mom giving me up.

As a grown woman, I now realize that it wasn't because my mother didn't love me. She just did what she had to do to make it easier for me, same as I did for my daughter. Sometimes life just brings us situations that we have no control over, and some things happen to make us see clearer. This situation gave me an urge deep down inside to want to see my mother, constantly I still wanted to know why.

The more I thought about it, the more I realized that it wasn't that she didn't love me, I know because I loved my daughter with all my heart, I was just so stressed out. As I took my time to sit back and think, I've come to grips that it was God's way of showing me things through His own eyes. I blamed myself for what I've done.

Everything in my life that was done wrong, I blamed myself. It didn't have to be my fault, different situations in my life steered me in the direction I needed to go.

Everyone has a story to tell, some stories have been known to help other people not to make the same mistakes as others have. A few years down the road, God answered my prayers.

Obstacles in My Way

The Bible talks about it being better to marry than to burn, but when you are not saved, you do not think about this, because we are set on doing our own thing. When I had my babies I didn't know what love really was. It was a feeling – sex that made me feel accepted . . . so I just let myself go without a thought. So every time I got pregnant I could not really blame the guy because I was not thinking past satisfying my own flesh. Out of all my children and what I went through, I know I love my kids. Knowing what I know now and the things that we experienced I would have been much more careful now that I am older and God has been so-o-o good. Most of my children have focus on their purpose in life and there is only a couple that I am praying that they will get their act together. I continually pray for all of them. No matter what we go through, if we keep our focus on God he will bring us through it.

My prayer was to finally get to see my biological mother. I finally got to ask her what I've been wanting for years. She told me the story on why she had to give me up. That's all I ever wanted was to hear that, and to know it wasn't my fault. God was my Savior; I was blessed with two families. I got the chance to meet my sisters and get to know them.

A few years after getting the chance to know them, my mom passed away. I had mixed emotions; I didn't know how to feel.

For some reason, I still felt like a part of me had died. My sisters were really hurt she was their only mother; me on the other hand I had one more. Having another mother wasn't the reason for my mixed emotions, I loved them both. I just didn't know what to feel. Taking you a few years back to when I got hooked up on drugs. I started off doing speed and acid. I'll never for get about the incident I had when I came in contact with LSD. I never tried that again.

As I look back and remember the people I used to do LSD, speed, and acid with, they never retrieved their minds. I know it wasn't anyone but God that kept me in my right mind. Eventually I was introduced to cocaine and later started free basing. After awhile my friends and I would get together after partying all night and go to this guys house. He used to sell us the drugs; we would hang out there for a while and get high as a kite.

Most of us would go home, while others would stay there all night. I had kids at home so I would try to leave around three or four in the morning. Even though they were old enough to stay home alone, I didn't like staying away from them like that. I would try to make it home before daybreak (that was my curfew).

I finally realized that God was in control, ordering my footsteps even when I still didn't acknowledge him. I gave everything else up and just started doing cocaine exclusively. I learned how to cook it and everything. It got so bad that every time I had money, I would spend it on getting high. Every payday I was not taking care of my business at all, selling food stamps to catch up and stuff. I would have my niece come over and I would give her some money and stamps to take my kids shopping for food and clothes. I know if I didn't I would just spend everything on cocaine. As time went on, still getting high; I became really weak, and half the time I didn't want to get out of bed.

It was so strange to me that one day something spoke to me and told me I had cancer, not realizing at that time the voice was really God. I eventually told my oldest daughter I had cancer, and her reply was "No You Don't"! I just told her ok. For many more months I continued on with my life, still getting high, until something within my soul revealed to me that I had cancer.

I decided to tell my other children about it. At that point it was urgent that I see a doctor. I still had not realized that something was really wrong, still not sure what. I know a majority of the people that find out they have cancer are afraid, but I wasn't, because I still wasn't sure. The enemy was trying to take me out of here. Thanks to God, he did not succeed.

Rapidly, I went from weighing 145lbs to 125lbs. The devil again was trying to destroy my life. When I finally got to the doctor, there were clots of blood seeping from inside of me. The nurse looked at me and said "OMG" I've never seen anything like this before; she advised me to get to the hospital immediately. I insisted that I needed to get a babysitter for my children. The truth is, my birthday was the next day; and all I had on my mind was getting high. I hung out and got high all day.

The next day I went to the hospital, I'm sure they found drug residue all in me, how can they not; even though they didn't say anything. But, I did find out that cancer of the uterus was eating at my body. I had to go through treatment and eventually I had a hysterectomy. Now I was headed for chemotherapy.

I missed my first treatment because I was getting high all night. My doctor called my sister advising her to tell me that I could not miss any more therapy sessions. At the time I hadn't even told my sister I had cancer, I really didn't think they cared.

She did care and she made sure I was at every session after that. I did not experience any pain during the cancer as people normally do. It must have been God again strengthening and protecting my body.

After months of chemotherapy, my daughter started attending services at this church where the pastor prayed for me. Eventually I started attending church on a regular basis. A friend from the church would always come to pick me up for service. Sometimes, if I had been getting high all night; when she came to get me I would hide, just so I wouldn't have to tell her I didn't want to go.

By this time God had completely healed my body from cancer, but I was still getting high. I will never forget I went to church on a Friday night. As the Pastor was preaching he made a statement; "if you have to put your drink and cocaine in your pocket don't stop coming to church". He said God will deliver you, if you just continue to come to church and trust in him. I knew he was speaking directly to me, that sermon stuck with me.

From that day on, God dealt with me more, and more, little by little. This started the process of my deliverance from drugs. I will never forget that night. I started attending regular services more often.

As time went by, my first position in the church was to usher. There was a funeral at the church. Another usher was with me, and she was battling with drugs also. It was something about that funeral service that gave me a desire to want to live.

When I returned home I called my sister and told her about the service. I was telling my sister how I felt because she was my prayer partner. As I was talking on the phone to her, something started happening. An unclean spirit manifested. My kids were telling me that my eyes turned bloodshot red. It was not me. My oldest daughter eventually got the phone away from me; my sister told her to go and get a bible and put it on my lap, and plead the blood of Jesus. I really don't remember too much about it, my daughter filled me in on what happened. My oldest daughter wasn't saved at the time, so she really couldn't help me. "Satan can't cast out Satan." I'm not calling my daughter Satan, but because she was not saved and full of the Holy Ghost, there was nothing she could have done for me.

I can say that she tried, after my sister told her to put the bible on my lap and plead the Blood of Jesus; the spirit told her that she didn't know anything about the blood. My daughter said; "I sure in the hell don't", and ran out of the house.

While my sister was still on the phone, she ended up calling my friend from the church; the one I would hide from when she would come to get me for church. She worked in the deliverance ministry. There was one other person that came first; she was much bigger than I was.

She was trying to hold me down, but that spirit in me was so strong, that she could not hold me down. My friend from the church finally got there. When I finally came to myself, it was about 11 pm, and I felt drained; but the next morning I felt free, I never touched any kind of drugs again. Don't think that the enemy didn't try to bring the smell of cocaine back to tempt me, but thank God I was totally delivered. Now 17 years later, from 1993 until now, I thank God I am drug free. I have overcome by the Blood of the Lamb and the word of my testimony.

Onward and Upward

That's why I tell you, even when we are not saved, God is still merciful in our lives, because there could have been a situation where they could have took my kids, but I was never evil or vindictive, which really did not matter. The word of God tells me when the enemy comes in like a flood that God will lift up a standard against him. Now this doesn't mean if you are out there; doing everything you think you are big and bad enough to do, and not doing your very best to take care of your home and your family, that God is going to just keep letting you mess up. My God has a way of letting you know, "Hey you better get yourself together or you are going to go through some things, because God is a jealous God. Being a Christian does not exempt you from going through and we do go through for different reasons, amen?! God is trying to help us to straighten up so that he can take us to another level of maturity in Him.

I just thank God I never had to go to any rehab or anything. I put all my trust in God and ran to him and not away from him. I learned from my trials that it easy to look for human help when you are in trouble. But is it the help that we need? Usually no one is there when you really need them.

One thing I realized is that God is always there when we need him. He may not come when you want him to, but he's always on time. If it had not been for the Lord on my side, I really don't know where I would be, or how my life would have turned out. Every situation I was in, he bailed me out. I've earned a great deal of respect for the man upstairs and for my life.

As the years continue to progress, I've noticed no one really has respect for each other these days. Most people don't respect themselves, so how can they respect someone else? They are quick to tell someone "I love you". God taught me to love and respect myself. Without him I probably wouldn't have respect for myself or anyone else either.

He also taught me not to look at myself as others do; but to look at myself through him, to love and respect myself as well as others. It took me many years to learn how to love myself; and many men in the process.

I really didn't know how to love, I was never taught that. I allowed lust to dictate how to feel about a man and the situation.

One thing I do know is that I loved my children, and with God's help and love, he allowed me to nurture my children as babies. I realize that you can tell a person all day long that you loved them, but saying and not showing is two different things. I can tell my children all day long that I love them, but if they don't feel it, then it's really not worth saying it. We have to love other's truthfully, not just for show, or because we want something.

When Jesus came down and allowed himself to be beaten and crucified, he did it for one reason only; so we would have eternal life and live it abundantly. When deliverance came into my life, it gave me freedom to live again; I now know what real love is. It was time for me to leave my familiar surroundings. I was still on the hunt for my family. God was giving me a new start and a new beginning.

I later found out that I had an aunt who lived in South Bend, Indiana. I didn't know them because my mother took me to Illinois when I was just three years old. I had never even heard of a South Bend, IN. God brought my aunt and her family in my life just in time, because I needed to get away.

At the time it was a set up for me to get to meet my biological mother. It was time for me to leave Illinois. I had lived there for over 30 years, and a few years in Louisiana.

So, for me to just pack up and move to a place that I had never even heard of was all God's plan for me. I went to talk to my pastor about thoughts of leaving; at first he said no, he didn't think it was a good idea. I wasn't so sure myself, but God put everything in motion for me. I also went to talk to my sister about it, and she said we should pray about it, and put it in God's hands. I talked to my children about it, and to my amazement; they all said "yes, we want to go". I was amazed because they were born and raised there, all of their family and friends were there; and that was all they knew, and they were willing to give it all up and go to a place where they knew nothing about. I ended up going to talk to my pastor again about it, and he agreed, it was our move. It was God.

The church gave us their blessing; they even took up a collection for us at service to help us with our new beginning. We left with only the clothes on our backs and two TV's, not knowing what was going to happen. I just put my faith in God, and allowed him to see us through. I left my three girls with my mother for about a month. I took my youngest son with me. I had to find us a place to live, and then I would return back for my girls.

I have never been separated from my children, so that month felt like a year. My son and I lived with my aunt for a little while. I started to look for my kids and me a place to live. God lead me to a place where they had some really nice town homes.

I went and filled out the application and everything, two days later I received a call and they told me I was approved for the town house. I didn't think I could afford that place with just me alone. I started taking things into my own hands. Then I thought to myself; why would they even approve me? I figured I could handle paying rent and bills easier. I had a job as a CNA, I just didn't think it was enough. It was really easy for me to get a job because I had good references from my first real job back home.

God had blessed me years before I left Illinois to leave the projects, and I know he doesn't take anyone backwards. I started thinking to myself I know the projects are not God's plan for me. Why would he take me from the projects of Illinois, just to put me back in the projects in Indiana? Since I was trying to do what was best for me and my kids instead of following God's plan, everything that could possibly go wrong, went wrong. I started having problems with my aunt that I was living with.

There was another guy that lived in South Bend, which I had known from Illinois; he allowed us to live with him until I found us a place to stay. My kids and I were all in one bedroom, roaches crawling all over the place.

By this time I had my girls with me also, we were running from place to place in the cold. It was my doing, not allowing God to lead, I was taking charge and messing up. School was getting ready to start, and it just seemed like time was running out for me. I was running in circles again, God dropped it in my spirit to go see the man that told me about the townhouses in the first place. So, I went back and asked her if she had any vacancies. She smiled at me and said yes. She went and got my application from the bottom of the pile, and gave me an apartment. All of that running around and I ended up back at the same place that God had originally had for me. Believe it or not, we survived there for 14 years.

All of my children graduated from high school and went onto college.

I even went back to get my GED, which took me four years to obtain. Math was the part I couldn't get; I ended up getting about four tutors to help me with math. Every time I thought I had it, I'd miss it by two points. I started to get really discouraged, and a few times I wanted to give up. God would not allow me to quit, so I kept going back and doing what ever I needed to do to pass that math. The third time was a charm.

I had a talk with God before I went in to take the test, and I told him; "Lord I am so tired of taking this test over and over again, and even if I don't get it this time, I would take it for as long as you want me to." I could only take the test so many times before I had to wait for a while to take it again. The woman that administered the test was a Christian. She saw how I kept coming back time after time. This time I took the test, it was a different feeling. I wasn't even worried if I had passed the test or not.

It was two days before Christmas; my kids had called me at work. The lady that had been given the test to me knew how important passing was to me. So, when the results came in; she bought them to my house directly. When my kids called they told me they had a surprise for me. They knew as well how important getting my GED was, and they were so happy.

On my way home from work, I was trying to figure out what they had for me; I was thinking maybe an early Christmas present. They handed me that manila folder, holding my GED certificate. I just started yelling; Oh My God! Oh My God! I passed, I passed, I started crying and thanking the Lord, I couldn't believe it. Finally I passed.

We had our ceremony where we received our diploma, the Mayor was there and everything. I was so proud of myself, but the most part of all is all my children were there. Yet another mountain overcome.

After getting my GED I didn't want to waist any more time, I had to figure out where to go from there. I was already in the nursing field, so I went to college and enrolled in some classes. I was able to get financial aid to pay for my classes, and I went through with the math and anatomy, taking the classes over and over again. I lost my financial aid due to my low scores.

This part of my life was good, but my personal life got crazy. I was trying to live my life as a saved woman, meaning free from all sin, with the help of God. Even though I firmly believe that every day we sin some kind of way. The bible tells us that if we say that we have not sinned, then we are liars. "We all fall short of the glory of God", that's what the bible says. The best part about falling short, we can always repent and ask for forgiveness, and to be honest about it and he will help us.

I fell short so many times due to fornication until I just knew I could never live that kind of life. I would find myself mad at myself every time I messed up, and vow never to see him again.

Another guy would come along and I would be right back at it again. My mind was telling me that I'm supposed to be a minister of the Lord. I was thinking God had made a mistake, because I wasn't living up to the standards of being a minister.

Never share your little secrets with anyone, because instead of people helping you overcome your shortcomings, they would hold them against you.

I had a good prayer partner, and I would share some things with her; and we would pray about them, she was truly a blessing in my life.

As I look back and realize the guys I was talking to; one was married, but I didn't know, and the other one was married but separated. I guess it was really no difference from me being a teenager, but I didn't want to live like that anymore. The one guy was always telling me how much he liked me and everything, but at the same time; why he couldn't get a divorce. Nevertheless, my God is real, He is true to his word, and he will answer your prayers.

I knew I needed help from God, especially if I was going to be strong enough to receive my deliverance. At the time, I didn't even know that the one guy was married. I was filing for bankruptcy, and he sent me to his lawyer for questions and concerns. Just in general conversation, he asked me where I knew the guy from.

"I couldn't just tell him we were sleeping partners." So, I just told him we went to school together, which wasn't a lie; because we did, that's where I met him. He was going to school to be a doctor's assistant, and I was going for practical nursing.

As I was talking to the lawyer; he says, "Oh yea, I have been knowing him and his wife for a long time". I said to myself "Wife?!" I couldn't wait until I left that office to get home and call him, and find out how come I didn't know he had a wife. He had all kinds of excuses about how, "she don't do this, and she don't do that", and how she neglects him. Even though we were together, his wife shouldn't have been a secret. It was another time we had hooked up, Valentine's Day, we went to a motel; and just everything he did was wrong. I'll never forget that day. I asked him, "Is this how you treat your wife"? So, to make a long story short, I got upset and went home. By this time I was really done with him. He was just so insensitive.

He called me the next morning, and I politely told him that, "you have a life with his wife and I need to get my own". At that time I really felt relieved. I was just thinking to myself, "one down, and one to go".

I wasn't seeing them both at the same time. The guy that was married, but separated, was the one I always ended up with when all else failed. He would always pop up at a weak moment in my life.

God was still dealing with me; I still needed to be delivered completely. I realize it was never anything but lust, because after I would get done, I would be upset and then I'd leave and go home. I didn't really like him the way he wanted me to.

He was a really nice guy, but it was some things I didn't appreciate from him, like using profanity in front of me. I wanted him to respect me because I was a minister, but how can I ask that if I'm fornicating with him?

I decided to tell him that I couldn't see him anymore, because this is not right, and I'm trying my best to live a righteous life for the Lord. He said he understood, but he still wasn't letting up. He would still call and ask me to go out to eat with him. I didn't see anything wrong with that.

I wanted a relationship, a real one, but I never had one; because I didn't know God. I wanted to have a relationship that God would approve of. He took me to this nice Italian restaurant a few times. He'd always have little mixed drinks that he would say, "don't have very much alcohol in them, or that you couldn't taste it". So, I decided to have soda pop instead. The next time we went that drink he ordered looked really good. So once again he said, "You can't taste the alcohol in it, and the waitress agreed with him". I decided to try it this time. It had been over 30 years since I had a drink.

That was one of the things I had been delivered from also. As soon as I tried that drink that looked so good, I taste the alcohol. He tried telling me that I was lying, and I didn't taste any alcohol, so I tried another sip.

Once again I could taste it, so I told him I didn't want anymore. He had already had two, so he took mine and drank it as well; then had the nerve to tell me that I embarrassed him. I know I had no business with him, or taking sips off that drink, I asked myself is this the guy for me?

A couple of weeks later he called me, and I reminded him how much of an embarrassment I was to him. He tried to change it as if he didn't mean it that way. "Well that's the way I took it" I just politely reminded him that I really had no business there with him anyway, and that I wasn't going to try and live that lifestyle.

I have chosen a different type of lifestyle, one that will make me happy. He then replied, "Well when you decide you want to see me, call me". That was the end of that lifestyle; I have lived a life that doesn't involve sex. If someone would have told me that I was going to go years without a man in my bed; "I would have told them they were crazy". God allowed me to just let him go, and move on.

My focus was back on school. It was time to take Anatomy and Math 050. It was really hard taking both classes at the same time. I took both classes about three times.

I ended up dropping one of those classes, which took my GPA down, and made it hard to receive financial aid for the next semester. I went to talk to my counselor about my classes. I had taken Physiology and passed; then that took my GPA back up a little, but not enough I thought.

I never returned to see if I could pick the classes back up that I had dropped. I was blessed that I had to pay $400, and take a qualified nursing assistance class. If I pass this class; I'd be making more money, and I would have had more responsibilities, like doing treatments and passing pills. I decided after praying about it, it wouldn't hurt trying.

I believe when God open doors for me, he will see me through it. I started my QMA classes; it was a lot to remember. I had to learn names of multiple pills and their side effects. It was such a challenge for me. I started to remember this verse from the bible, "If God is for me, then who can be against me"? During training, I paired up with this Asian girl; she was there to be a registered nurse. She used to ask me all kinds of questions, like what did I get for this answer, and what did I get for that answer?

I thought of all people, she was asking me. She had a lot on her plate, so it was really good for me to be a blessing to her any way I could.

The classes were very intense, but I was finally done, I made it through. It was a three step process. The first step was the class itself;

the 40 hours of training, and last the test. The training wasn't really hard, because I had been in the nursing field for a while now. Being a QMA was a big step for me, very different from what I had been doing. I never thought I'd be able to pass pills.

I normally just wash the residents up, give them a bath, feed them, make beds; the regular stuff. There's really no class needed to learn how that works. So, I started training on passing pills and giving treatments. When I started training it was like an entire different ball game for me. I had much bigger responsibilities.

I had to make sure the right person had the right medication, the right dosage and the whole nine yards. It was very important that I pay close attention to what I was reading. It didn't take long at all. The more and more I practiced, the faster I learned.

My forty hours were done, and now it was time for the test. I prayed and prayed, and studied and studied until I thought my head was going to explode. I had so many long words to learn, it seemed like none of it was coming into focus for me.

The truth is I know God will bring it all back to me, as long as I work at it. I studied everything because I wasn't sure what all was going to be on the test.

Finally, the big day was here. We took our test the same day as the C.N.A's took theirs. Well, I failed the test, so, I had to go to the instructor and let her know I didn't pass and figure out what the next step was.

I was so disappointed, all the time I was studying; I was studying the wrong words. I had two months to studying before I could retake the test again. Meanwhile I continued to study; I decided to talk to my pastor about it. He told me that God is with me and so was he. That little message stuck with me all week, it was time to take the test again.

In the back of my mind I could hear my pastor's voice, it was awesome. As I was sitting there again, waiting for the C.N.A.'s to finish their test. I said to myself, "God I wish they would hurry up so I can take my test". Immediately after I said that, the instructor looked over at me and told me, it wouldn't be much longer.

I felt the presence of God like never before. I began to recite this prayer, "God if you could just bless me to allow at least the words and side effects that I already remember be on this test, I think I'll be ok". This test was totally different from the first test I had taken. It looked as if it was so much easier to read and understand. The questions on the test were exactly what I had asked for. Most of the pills they asked about were the ones I remember. The few words that I didn't know I just used the process of elimination and was able to answer the questions.

I finished the test and took it to the instructor. As I sat and waited for her to grade my test, I had such a peace come upon me that I can't even describe. It was such a good feeling. An 80 percent or better was needed to pass. The instructor called my name, I went over to her; she looked at me and said congratulations. I grabbed that instructor and gave her the biggest hug, I was so ecstatic, everyone was happy for me. I was thanking God over and over. I just went and sat in my car to collect my thoughts.

When I called my daughter to tell her what happened, tears rolled down my face. She asked me, "Why was I crying?" I told her I was so overwhelmed and thankful to God, he blessed me once again to overcome a mountain. Thank You Lord! Next step was hoping my job uses me as a QMA sometimes, so I can get use to my new position.

I had been working at this particular nursing home for a year now, but I have been a C.N.A. for about twelve years; and everyone seems to think I'm good at what I do. I wanted to be an even better QMA. They started me off on the graveyard shift, 11pm-7am. I really didn't like that shift because I was always sleepy, but I had to do what I had to do.

I figured if I do well on the night shift, they would eventually use me in the daytime. God had another plan for me. They were using me more as a C.N.A., but it was ok because I was getting the QMA pay. At first I felt they really didn't want to give me a chance, the hired a full time QMA. This one lady I met had told me about this other residential facility, which hired QMA's only. So, I went over there, filled out the application and got hired.

The Director of Nursing was so understanding with the fact that I had just got certified, that she agreed to work with me. I was so nervous, it seemed like it took me forever to just pass pills. The really bad part about it was I knew no one there. Knowing the people would have made it a little easier for me. God had given me favor with my boss already. I made one big mistake where they had to call me at home. I thought I was going to lose my certification already, but everything worked out alright.

I have been at my job for over a year now, and I've gotten much better and more relaxed. As I sit here and think about my life right now, wandering if I want to go back to school and be a nurse now or what. I'm fifty-eight years old now, so I really need to decide. I'm just still not sure. I just pray and seek God for guidance; which ever way he leads me, I will follow.

God always opens doors, ok? I pray that if you are reading this book, that you will come to trust in God and don't be in a hurry, because God will never fail us. One thing I've learned through all of my accomplishments is that, if we trust God with all our hearts, even when things don't look so good for us, we can't give up. Knowing and trusting that if God have brought you this far, he will take you the rest of the way. We just can't give up, because God has already made the way. He just wants us to trust him on this journey, and give him the glory.

I thank God for all he has done for me and my family. God has bought us through many mountains that I never thought we would get through. What you have read is a true, heart wrenching story about a young lady overcoming every obstacle that came her way, by the Grace of God.

-Ozell Wilson

This is my prayer for you, that in this life we go through many hurts of the past, present, and future... but if we are honest with ourselves, that we have been wounded in many areas of our lives . . . God can bring the deliverance and healing we so desperately need. I encourage you to live committed to God, free and productive in every area of your life. Be blessed, be healed, be delivered in the name of our Lord Jesus Christ.

There is so much more that God has done and it still doing in my life, I just pray that whatever you are going through, allow God to help you. He can, and he will. If you have not given your life to God today is the day. Not only give him your life, love him, you will see that your life will never be the same. Trust God.

I know that I have only just begun the process that the Sovereign Lord has called me to do. He called me to do the work of an Evangelist, helping others to accept the Lord Jesus Christ as their personal Lord and Savior. What he has done for me; the work that he has begun, through many mountains that I had to climb, and through the valleys that He brought me out of – I am sure that where he has brought me from, he can do the same for you, if you trust and believe in HIM.

Psalms 121:1-2
I will lift up my eyes to the hills, from whence comes my help, my help comes from the Lord, who made heaven and earth.

1 Peter 2:9 You are a chosen, generation, a royal priesthood, a holy nation, his own special people, that you may proclaim the praises of Him who called you out of darkness into his marvelous light.

Romans 8:28-30. And we know that all things work together for good, to those who love God, to those who are called according to his purpose. For whom he forknew, he also predestined to be conformed to the image of His son, that he might be the firstborn among many brethren.

Moreover, whom he predestined these he also called; whom he called, these he also justified; and whom he justified these he also glorified.

Isaiah 60:1 Arise, shine; for your light has come! And the Glory of the Lord has risen upon you.

Every time we go through something the enemy (devil) will always be there to try and make us think that his way is better. So if his way was so much better, why did he get kicked out of Heaven, why did I get hooked on cocaine, why did I wind up in jail for stabbing that man . . . Why? . , why. . , did the devil send that man to rape me? The devil comes to steal, kill, and destroy . . . Jesus came that we may have life ... more abundantly. It is not God's will to hurt us that is satan's job. So I know the devil came to bring more fear into my life. I can see how if I had never let go of any of the hurt in my life satan would continue to set me up to fail. This book will help you to not let the devil have so much power over you. He can put things on our path to detour us, by making things look very enticing. Know that we have to make a choice whether we are going to take that step or not in the right or wrong direction.

The more we understand that our Heavenly Father has made a way of escape from every snare that the enemy has set for us, the greater one inside of us will enable us to walk by faith allowing him to have His way in our lives to work for us.

About The Author

Ozell Wilson is a single mom, who is a mother, grandmother, great-grandmother. She works as a QMA. She is active in her church as a minister of the Gospel. Her goal is to encourage women to get the best out of their life.

I thank God for Elder JoAnn Walker who was very instrumental in helping to prepare this book. And again I thank all my children and grandchildren for encouraging me to move ahead and put my life out there. Hoping and praying that someone will be encouraged, knowing that there is a way out of everything that life brings their way. God bless.

My foster mother died at age 101. A week before her 102nd birthday. I do thank God for her. If only she were able to see the finishing of this book. I love you mom.

May God fill you with his love, every day as you trust in him, by the Power of the Holy Spirit. Be blessed

www.ingramcontent.com/pod-product-compliance
Lightning Source LLC
Chambersburg PA
CBHW022214090526
44584CB00013BA/906